GENESIS 1-11

CW01664160

BEYOND EDEN

9 INTERACTIVE BIBLE STUDIES FOR SMALL GROUPS AND INDIVIDUALS

PHILLIP D. JENSEN AND TONY PAYNE

matthiasmedia

NB

Beyond Eden
Second edition

First published 1990

Matthias Media
(St Matthias Press Ltd ACN 067 558 365)
PO Box 225
Kingsford NSW 2032
Australia
Telephone: (02) 9663 1478; international: +61-2-9663-1478
Facsimile: (02) 9663 3265; international: +61-2-9663-3265
Email: info@matthiasmedia.com.au
Internet: www.matthiasmedia.com.au

Matthias Media (USA)
Telephone: 724 964 8152; international: +1-724-964-8152
Facsimile: 724 964 8166; international: +1-724-964-8166
Email: sales@matthiasmedia.com
Internet: www.matthiasmedia.com

ISBN 978 1 921441 68 4

Cover design and typesetting by Lankshear Design Pty Ltd.

» CONTENTS

» HOW TO MAKE THE MOST OF THESE STUDIES

1. A Christian approach to Genesis

To begin at the beginning …

The beginning seems an obvious place to start, but many Christians are ignorant of the message of the opening chapters of the Bible. Genesis 1-11 may be familiar to us because of the well-known events it relates—Creation, the creation of Adam and Eve, the Fall, Cain and Abel's rivalry, Noah's calling and the Flood—but what is its *meaning*?

When we do turn to these chapters, we find ourselves swamped by controversy. How long did Creation take? Were Adam and Eve real people? Where did Cain's wife come from? Was Methuselah's 969-year life span the same as 969 of our modern years?

Unfortunately our interest in these questions of historical detail tends to distract us from what Genesis 1-11 is really about. By asking the wrong questions, we come up with the wrong answers.

In particular, we lose sight of the place that Genesis has in the history of God's dealings with the world. Genesis sets the scene. In eleven short chapters, it describes how the world came to be the way it is, and what we should expect as God sets in motion his plan of redemption.

The nine studies in this book offer a *Christian* interpretation of Genesis 1-11. They read Genesis from the perspective of Christ, who is the linchpin in God's unfolding plan. Christ is the key that unlocks the meaning of these eleven momentous chapters.

By looking at Genesis in this way (the way that, in fact, we should read all of the Bible), we hope that you will learn not only what Genesis is saying, but what the whole Bible is saying.

2. What is an Interactive Bible Study?

Interactive Bible Studies are a bit like a guided tour of a famous city. They take you through a particular part of the Bible, helping you to know where to start, pointing out things along the way, suggesting avenues for further exploration, and making sure that you know how to get home. Like any good tour, the real purpose is to allow you to go exploring for yourself—to dive in, have a good look around, and discover for yourself the riches that God's word has in store.

In other words, these studies aim to provide stimulation and input and point you in the right direction, while leaving you to do plenty of the exploration and discovery yourself.

We hope that these studies will stimulate lots of 'interaction'—interaction with the Bible, with the things we've written, with your own current thoughts and attitudes, with other people as you discuss them, and with God as you talk to him about it all.

3. The format

Each study contains four main components:

- short sections of text that introduce, inform, summarize and challenge
- a set of numbered study questions that help you examine the passage and think through its meaning
- an 'Implications' section that helps you think about

what this passage means for you and your life today
- suggestions for thanksgiving and prayer as you close.

4. How to use these studies on your own

- Before you begin, pray that God would open your eyes to what he is saying in the Bible, and give you the spiritual strength to do something about it.
- Work through the study, reading the text and answering the questions about the Bible passage.
- Resist the temptation to skip over the 'Implications' and 'Give thanks and pray' sections at the end. It is important that we not only hear and understand God's word, but respond to it. These closing sections help us do that.
- Take what opportunities you can to talk to others about what you've learnt.

5. How to use these studies in a small group

- Much of the above applies to group study as well. The studies are suitable for structured Bible study or cell groups, as well as for more informal pairs and triplets. Get together with a friend or friends and work through them at your own pace; use them as the basis for regular Bible study with your spouse. You don't need the formal structure of a 'group' to gain maximum benefit.
- For small groups, it is *very useful* if group members can work through the study themselves *before* the group meets. The group discussion can take place comfortably in an hour (depending on how sidetracked you get!) if all the members have done some work in advance.
- The role of the group leader is to direct the course of the discussion and to try to draw the threads together at the end. This will mean a little extra preparation—underlining the sections of text to emphasize and read out loud, working out which questions are worth concentrating on, and being sure of the main thrust of the study. Leaders will also probably want to work

out approximately how long they'd like to spend on each part.

- If your group members usually don't work through the study in advance, it's extra important that the leader prepares which parts to concentrate on, and which parts to glide past more quickly. In particular, the leader will need to select which of the 'Implications' to focus on.
- We haven't included an 'answer guide' to the questions in the studies. This is a deliberate move. We want to give you a guided tour of the Bible, not a lecture. There is more than enough in the text we have written and the questions we have asked to point you in what we think is the right direction. The rest is up to you.

6. Bible translation

Previous editions of this Interactive Bible Study have assumed that most readers would be using the New International Version of the Bible. However, since the release of the English Standard Version in 2001, many have switched to the ESV for study purposes. So with this new edition of *Beyond Eden*, we have decided to quote from and refer to the ESV text, which we recommend.

» STUDY 1

IN THE BEGINNING

[GENESIS 1:1-2:3]

Our questions

When we approach the first book of the Bible—especially its first few chapters—there are always questions on our lips. Were the seven days of Creation seven 24-hour days? Does the order of Creation square with modern theories about the evolution of species? Is there a basic conflict between science and Christianity? Is this creation account a space-time event, or a myth intended to convey a purely religious meaning?

There has been fierce controversy surrounding these questions. The atheists hurl barbs at the 'head-in-sand' creationists; the creationists retaliate by exploiting the gaps in evolutionary theory. Other Christians distance themselves from the creationists, arguing that the integrity of Genesis can be maintained without a 24-hour-day, 4004 BC Creation. And on it goes. More importantly, in evangelism, we trade arguments about carbon dating and the latest archaeological finds, and Jesus is lost in a sea of quasi-scientific confusion.

As we begin to study Genesis, we cannot help but have these concerns in our minds—concerns that owe more to biology and astronomy than the Bible. While these questions are certainly legitimate, we must take care that they do not obscure the real message of Genesis. The key to all good research, including Bible research, is asking the *right* questions. If we try to find answers to *our* questions in Genesis—questions that Genesis does not answer—our search will be fruitless. We do not consult a street directory to find phone numbers; nor should we consult Genesis to find answers to questions it is not the least concerned to answer.

Moreover, if we are too obsessed with modern controversy, we may overlook the searching questions that Genesis is asking *us*. These are questions of far greater moment than the details of some primeval chemical reaction. They are questions about the very nature of our lives. Does life have meaning? Do we, as persons, have any meaning? Should we think of ourselves as 'persons', or merely as apes who have learned to walk? But more of this in due time.

Firstly, let us turn to the text and examine it more closely.

Read Genesis 1:1-2:3.

1. Summarize the main ideas under the following headings:

- God

- The creation

- Man

- Any other observations

As you looked at the passage, you might have noticed the following things.

1. A structured account

ONE OF THE FIRST THINGS WE NOTICE about this passage is its highly patterned structure. The account unfolds in a repetitive, orderly fashion, reflecting God's deliberate, orderly work of creation. It is a structured account of the structuring of the world.

The pattern is broken at verse 26 with the creation of man. Is this the climax of the account? Is the seventh day an anticlimax?

2. God

God dominates the passage as he dominates his creation. He is mentioned 35 times—initiating, speaking, working, creating, blessing, resting. He is the subject of all the action. In fact, the emphasis of the passage could be summarized by its first four words: "In the beginning, God …"

We should note three things:

a) God creates everything, both large and small

Nothing is outside the scope of God's work. There is nothing 'natural' in the sense of being beyond his creative work. The world is his. He made it—all of it.

b) He creates in an orderly and purposeful way

God does not create arbitrarily or on a whim. Nor is he haphazard. He creates an orderly world in which we can live orderly, purposeful lives. The prophet Isaiah says:

> … the LORD,
> who created the heavens
> (he is God!),
> who formed the earth and made it
> (he established it;
> he did not create it empty,
> he formed it to be inhabited!) …
> (Isa 45:18)

The word 'empty' in Isaiah is the same word used in Genesis 1:2 (translated 'void' in the ESV). As God sees that his world is habitable, God is pleased. He looks at it and sees that it is good.

c) God creates by his word

Although very little is said about the mechanism of creation, one important thing is said repeatedly: "And God said …" The details are unimportant—even irrelevant.

The important thing is that God has only to speak and things come into being.

This is true of any powerful person. If the Prime Minister speaks, things happen. If he decrees that a highway should be built, it will be done. The details of who actually does the dirty work are unimportant. The PM will say, quite rightly, "I built that road".

God, who appoints Prime Ministers to do *his* dirty work, brings matter out of nothing simply by a word. What sort of awesome figure is this? It is hard for us to conceive of a power this great. "By the word of the LORD the heavens were made, and by the breath of his mouth all their host" (Ps 33:6).

3. Creation

The creation reflects the character of its creator, and fulfils the purpose for which he made it.

a) The creation is dependent on its creator

This may seem to be stating the obvious, but in our current climate, it needs to be said: our world is not self-generating or self-sustaining; it owes its existence and its continued operation to the will of the creator.

Because of the order and predictability that God has built into our world, we are often tempted to think of it as a giant machine that runs on forever, going through the cycle of the seasons with comforting regularity. But we only have to pause and consider the frailty of our own lives to realize how dependent we really are. A microscopic virus can cut short our lives in a few days or weeks. The food supply we take for granted is generated by others; we are dependent on them, and they, in turn, are dependent on the seasons and the weather for a successful yield. Ultimately, it all depends on God.

b) The creation is orderly and habitable

Our orderly, investigable world ecosystem was created and is sustained by a divinely reasonable being. God intended it to be habitable, and it was so.

As with many of the themes of Genesis, we can fail to grasp the implications of this idea. Our whole view of the world is based on this concept of an orderly, reasonable creation. Other cultures have regarded the world as a chaotic, nightmarish place, formed through the chance sexual encounter of some god with some goddess. Western civilization, in contrast, has developed in a world that is understood to be orderly.

c) The creation is good

The repetition of this phrase throughout the passage should leave us in no doubt that our world, as created by God, is very good. This, too, is a civilization-changing concept: the created world is not an evil thing or a distraction, to be cast off as we become more spiritual. Nor is it an illusion, as many eastern religions (along with the Christian Scientists) believe. It is real, and separate from its creator, and decidedly good.

4. Man

With the creation of man (that is, mankind) in verse 26, the highly structured pattern changes. Is this just another of God's creatures, or is there something different happening?

a) Man is a dependent creature

Like the rest of the creation, man owes his genesis to God. He does not rise by chemical chance from the primordial slime; he too springs from the creator's mind, will and word.

This is tremendously important for our self-perception. We like to think of ourselves as persons—as somehow more significant than other creatures. Moreover, we want to think that our lives have some purpose—some meaning. Yet without the creative work of God, our lives have no meaning. If we are but a biological accident, how can we hope to have any purpose? An accident, by definition, is devoid of purpose; it just happens.

For there to be purpose and meaning, there must be manufacture. This is deeply offensive to us humans—especially 21st-century humans. We hate the idea that we are made by someone else, are dependent on someone else, and are given purpose and meaning by someone else. Yet we cannot face the alternative—that we are an absurd accident, a cosmic joke occasioned by time plus matter plus chance.

b) Man is unique

We will look at this in more detail in the second study; suffice to say at this point that man is created in God's image to rule over the rest of the creation. Does man have any dignity? Is whaling murder? Is abortion murder? These questions all swing on our view of mankind, and in the next study, we will look in more detail at what Genesis has to say about this.

5. Christ

There is another theme here, too, lurking just below the surface. Who does God consult with in verse 26 when he says, "Let us make man in our image"? Is he just using the royal plural? Or is there another divine figure involved in creation?

This becomes clearer as the Scriptures unfold.

Read John 1:1-14.

2. What parallels do you see with Genesis 1?

3. Who is God's creative "Word" (v. 1)?

Read Colossians 1:15-17.

4. How was Jesus involved in the creation of the world?

5. Why was the world created?

6. Alternatives

The value of what God is saying in Genesis becomes even more apparent when we consider the alternatives.

Ancient alternatives

We cannot know whether the author of Genesis had particular alternatives in mind. Certainly, he cuts across many of the ideas of the ancient world:

- *Astrology*: Many ancient civilizations were convinced that the stars played a dominant role in human affairs. Genesis 1 blows a raspberry at this idea. The stars are not our masters, but our servants; they are part of the creation over which man has dominion.
- *Polytheism*: There is no room in Genesis for a rash of gods each doing a bit here and there; there is only one God (the involvement of Christ notwithstanding).
- *The seventh day*: It is interesting to note that in Mesopotamia, the seventh day was regarded as a day of ill—a day of foreboding and evil omen. In Genesis, it is the best day of all—the day when God rests, the day that God blesses and calls holy.

Modern alternatives

Current alternatives to the Genesis view of the world abound. Here are but a few:

- *Astrology*: Quite astonishingly, many people still believe in the influence of the stars. 80 per cent of Australians read their star column, and 28 per cent profess to believe what it says. From a scientific, or astronomical, point of view, the whole thing is a fraud. Yet many still cling to it.
- *Mysticism*: This is the idea that the physical world is an evil place and that true spirituality involves escaping the captivity of our physical environment to soar into the great spiritual unknown. The concept is as old as Plato, who distinguished between body and soul—the soul being the true and immortal principle, and the body being a hindrance. There has been a revival of this thinking in the western world thanks to the spread of eastern mystic religion (e.g. the Hare Krishnas and transcendental meditation). In this system, the physical world is not simply evil; it is an illusion that inhibits our spiritual progress. In this kind of system, there is little place for physical beauty or sexual pleasure. In God's world, the physical matter is good, not evil, and sex is to be enjoyed!
- *Materialism*: This is a WYSIWYG world view (What You See Is What You Get). The world is a closed system in the sense that there is no God outside the creation. There is only matter—matter that was once highly concentrated, then exploded with a Big Bang, formed itself into life, and keeps expanding through the endless reaches of space. As we have noted earlier, in this alternative, meaning, purpose and values are disposed of, along with God. The honest materialist will eat, drink and be merry, for tomorrow he may die, and beyond that, there is nothing.

Genesis might not answer all our questions, but it does have some important questions to ask *us*. Here are just a few to get you thinking.

» Implications

(Choose one or more of the following to think about further or to discuss in your group.)

- What sort of God do we meet in Genesis 1?

- How should we respond to this God?

- Who are you (as a human being)? What are you like?

- What is the purpose of the creation?

- What is the purpose behind *your* creation? What is your life about?

» Give thanks and pray

- Praise God for creating the world to be ordered, structured, purposeful and good through Christ and for Christ.
- Thank God for creating humankind. Thank him in particular for creating you.
- Ask him to help you to respond to him appropriately as the creator of the world and everything in it.
- Ask him to give you the wisdom to know what to say as you talk to non-Christians about the meaning and purpose of life.

» STUDY 2

GOD'S IMAGE: RULE

[GENESIS 1:26-28]

DEEP DOWN, MANKIND IS BASICALLY evil. Deep down, mankind is basically good.

For centuries, thinkers have argued about which of these two opposing statements is true.

1. Write down the evidence you would use if you had to argue for each side.

    - Man is good

    - Man is evil

A GOOD CASE CAN BE MADE FOR EACH, and this is not surprising because (in a sense) both are true. Mankind is a puzzle: we are capable of the most admirable thoughts and deeds, and the most barbaric evil.

The ancient Greek playwright Sophocles is remembered by the *Oxford Dictionary of Quotations* for just two sayings: "Wonders are many, and none is more wonderful than man" and "Not to have been born is best". This is the paradox of man: we are the glory of the world, but the garbage as well. We are just a speck of dust in a vast universe, yet we dominate our world and build spacecraft to travel to the very stars that dwarf us. Just who or what are we—we human beings? Are we particularly complex and vicious animals? Or are we much, much more?

The author of Psalm 8 pondered this too:

> When I look at your heavens, the work of your fingers,
> the moon and the stars, which you have set in place,
> what is man that you are mindful of him,
> and the son of man that you care for him?
>
> Yet you have made him a little lower than the heavenly beings
> and crowned him with glory and honor. (Ps 8:3-5)

Perhaps the most important statement in the Bible about mankind is in Genesis 1:26-28—that we have been created in the image of God. But what does it mean for us to be 'in the image of God'?

There have been many suggestions. These verses have become a sort of all-purpose proof text for many modern doctrines and controversies. The phrase 'image of God' is seemingly so broad. What is unique about man that he can be said to be in God's image? Is it his soul, his spiritual potential, his capacity for rational thought, his ability to speak, his appearance, his innate moral sense, his responsibility for the world, or a chop suey of some or all of these?

As with all these studies, we will try to discover what the *Bible* makes of Genesis. What does the rest of the Bible take 'the image of God' to mean? Amid all the competing interpretations, there is only one that we can trust: the Bible's own.

'The image' in Genesis

Genesis 1:26-28 does not precisely define what is meant by man being in the image of God. However, when we look carefully at these verses, two concepts are involved.

The first is *rule*:

> "Let us make man in our image, after our likeness. And let them have dominion over the fish of the sea and over the birds of the heavens and over the livestock and over all the earth and over every creeping thing that creeps on the earth." (v. 26)

Man is to be God's representative ruler on earth. Man is like God in that he rules the earth, as God does. God restates this as he blesses the man and woman in verse 28: "Be fruitful and multiply and fill the earth and subdue it and have dominion over the fish of the sea ..." At the very least, then, man being in the 'image of God' involves ruling the world.

But there is a second important theme, which we might call *relationship*. In verses 26-27, God is both singular (God, he, his) and plural (us, our). It is not surprising, then, that when man is created in God's image, he too is both singular and plural:

> So God created man in his own image,
> in the image of God he created him;
> male and female he created them. (v. 27)

Like God, mankind is both unified and diverse. We know from the rest of Scripture that the three persons of the Godhead (Father, Son and Holy Spirit) are nevertheless a single God, and that from all eternity, they have enjoyed relationship with each other. Mankind is created in this image, with separate persons (male and female) created to enjoy a deep unity. This idea is developed in chapter 2, where the man and his wife are united and become "one flesh" (2:24).

In Genesis 1:26-28, then, the 'image of God' involves *rule* and *relationship*.

2. In the rest of Genesis, the word 'image' occurs only twice. Look up these references and see what light they cast on the meaning of 'image of God'.

- Genesis 5:1-3

- Genesis 9:6

The effect of the Fall

IT IS ALSO WORTH NOTING THAT mankind is still regarded as being made in God's image after the Fall. The eruption of sin in the lives of Adam and Eve destroyed their harmony with God, each other and the world, but it did not wipe out the image of God that they bore.

If the 'image of God' involves rule and relationship (Gen 1:26-28), then we can see that these two attributes remain after the Fall, but in a tainted, tarnished state. Man still rules the world, and yet fails to. The ground is now hostile (thorns, sweat etc.—see Genesis 3). Because of his sin, man rules poorly, unjustly, tragically. He also maintains his capacity for relationship, but it, too, is marred and broken.

The image is still there, but it is flawed.

In the rest of the Old Testament

In the rest of the Old Testament, the word 'image' occurs quite frequently, but only in reference to the idols or 'images' of Israel's pagan neighbours. The attitude to these idols is consistent: as 'images of God', they are hopeless. How can a statue that is dead and that cannot speak represent, in any way, the true and living God who talks to his people? This is what God says about idols through the prophet Isaiah:

> To whom will you liken me and
> make me equal,
> and compare me, that we may
> be alike?
> Those who lavish gold from the
> purse,
> and weigh out silver in the scales,
> hire a goldsmith, and he makes it
> into a god;
> then they fall down and worship!
> They lift it to their shoulders, they
> carry it,
> they set it in its place, and it
> stands there;
> it cannot move from its place.
> If one cries to it, it does not answer
> or save him from his trouble.
> (Isa 46:5-7)

In the New Testament

The ideas we have seen in the Old Testament are either repeated or developed in the New Testament. James 3:9 echoes the sentiments of Genesis 9:6 that man, since he is made in the image of God, should be treated with respect. In James, the example given is cursing: how can we curse or insult something (or someone) who has been made in God's image?

The idolatry theme is also taken up. Christianity is characterized by turning away from idols to serve the true and living God (1 Thess 1:9). It is also interesting that the definition of idolatry is broadened to include covetousness in Colossians 3:5, because it involves worshipping created things rather than the creator.

However, the most significant developments are in the twin themes we saw in Genesis 1:26-28—rule and relationship. In both cases, Christ plays a crucial role. In the rest of this study, we will look at the 'rule' theme and save the 'relationship' idea for our next study.

In the New Testament, Christ is *the* image of God. This is where the 'image of God' theme is really developed and finds its fulfilment. But in what sense is Jesus the image of God? How does this relate to man being made in God's image? Is it of any relevance? Let us try to answer these questions by studying Hebrews 2:5-10 (with brief reference to Colossians 1:15 and Hebrews 1:3).

Read Hebrews 2:5-10.

3. Where is the quote in verses 6-8 taken from? What point is the writer of Hebrews making in these verses?

4. Is this a true reflection of the world as we know it? Explain.

5. Who *is* ruling then (according to verse 9)?

6. List what Colossians 1:15-17 and Hebrews 1:1-3 say about Jesus.

(NB: By the first century, the word 'firstborn' (used in Colossians 1:15) had come to mean 'heir', as in the 'first born' son who, in the ancient world, inherited his father's estate.)

7. Back to Hebrews 2:5-10. If Jesus is now the ruler (rather than man), how does that fit with Genesis 1:26-28 where man is supposed to rule the earth? (Look especially at Hebrews 2:9, 14; also look up 1 Corinthians 15:45-49.)

8. Jesus is now the risen ruler, "crowned with glory and honor" (Heb 2:9). But is he still a man?

Let us look further at how the 'image of God' theme relates to us as Christians. There are three aspects to it.

a) We've put on a new self

Colossians 3:9-10 says,

> Do not lie to one another, seeing that you have put off the old self with its practices and have put on the new self, which is being renewed in knowledge after the image of its creator.

The image that was marred by the Fall—the old self with all its destructive, antisocial practices—has now been "put off" by Christians. There has been a radical change. We have said 'No' to our old way of life; we have made a decisive, 180-degree change in direction. The "new self" we have put on begins the process of restoring the tainted image. It is being "renewed in knowledge after the image of its creator".

b) We keep being transformed

This work is not yet complete. The decisive change has been made, the direction has been set, but the transformation goes on gradually throughout our Christian lives:

> And we all, with unveiled face, beholding the glory of the Lord, are being transformed into the same image from one degree of glory to another. For this comes from the Lord who is the Spirit. (2 Cor 3:18)

Our bodies continue to decay, but the image—the likeness—grows day by day. In other words, in this present age, the change is spiritual, not physical: "Though our outer self is wasting away, our inner self is being renewed day by day" (2 Cor 4:16).

c) One day it will all be complete

When Christ comes again in glory, the process will be over:

> But our citizenship is in heaven, and from it we await a Savior, the Lord Jesus Christ, who will transform our lowly body to be like his glorious body, by the power that enables him even to subject all things to himself. (Phil 3:20-21)

At that time, we will be transformed to be like Jesus, spiritually *and* physically. He is *the* image of God—the man who rules the creation. At that time, we too, his brothers whom he purchased by his death, will rule with him, as we were created to.

Summary

These are difficult ideas. Let's try to summarize them.

a) Man as created

Man is created by God in his image. In Genesis 1, the 'image of God' involves man ruling the creation (like God) and being a diverse being in relationship with his fellow men (like God). As the Bible unfolds, and especially with the coming of Christ, these themes are developed.

Although man has been created in God's image to rule the world, we fail because of our sin. Here lies the paradox of man: we are just a little lower than the angels, and yet we are a dismal failure in our relationships with God, each other and our environment.

b) Jesus, the man

Jesus is man as God meant him to be—a man in God's image, ruling the world. Jesus is truly a man (and so fulfils Genesis 1), yet is untainted by sin and failure. He is the exact representation of God—a perfect image—and he rules and inherits all God's creation (Col 1:15ff; Heb 1:2-3).

Furthermore, this was how God planned it from the beginning. The world was made so that Christ would inherit it (Col 1:16; Eph 1:9-10).

c) Man re-created

Part of this mind-boggling plan was that mankind could become what we were created to be. Christ assumes his place on the throne by dying as man and rising as man, and this was for our sake—that he might bring us to glory as well (Heb 2:10, 14). Because he has dealt with our sin (through his death and resurrection), we can be renewed; we can become like our creator; we can reverse the tragic consequences of the Fall, and we can once more rule the world in harmony with God, each other and the world.

This process has already begun in Christians. We are being transformed into God's likeness day by day. The process will be completed on the last day when our bodies will also be changed to be like Christ's glorious resurrection body.

Ruling today

The consequences and implications of these ideas are vast. There are numerous issues that are affected by the Bible's view of man. The first and most obvious is that human life is of value. As creatures who bear God's image, we have real worth, and are to be treated with appropriate dignity and respect. All kinds of human oppression, racism and exploitation are not only crimes against justice, but crimes against the worth and dignity of us as God's image-bearers.

The place of man in the world is also determined by Genesis 1:26-28. Environmental issues are high on the social agenda these days, and Christians have a lot to contribute to the discussion. We are, perhaps, the only group that actually has a coherent rationale for looking after the earth and its resources. It has been placed in our care by God; we are to rule over it, and so have responsibility for it. It is a cruel caricature of Genesis 1-2 to suggest that our dominion over God's good earth is a licence to degrade and exploit it. However, God does place man at the apex of the created order, and he gives creation to him to subdue and to prosper in.

Genesis 1, and Christ's fulfilment of it, also helps us see what it means to be fully human. What is a real man? What is a real woman? The answer to both of these questions is: a Christian—one who is gradually becoming like Christ, the perfect man.

» Implications

(Choose one or more of the following to think about further or to discuss in your group.)

- Given Genesis 1, what attitude do you think Christians should have towards environmentalism?

- What could you say to friends or family when the subject of environmentalism arises in conversation?

- From what we have looked at, what is God's plan for your life? (Another way of putting it is: what is the purpose or goal of your life?)

- Write down three ways in which God's plan for your life should affect you in practical terms.

  1.

  2.

  3.

» Give thanks and pray

- Thank God for creating you in his image for rule and relationship.
- Thank him especially for Jesus, the perfect man who lived the way God meant us to live. Thank God for sending Jesus to deal with our sin through his death and resurrection so that we can truly take on God's likeness.
- Ask God to work in you day by day to make you more like Christ as you put off the old self and put on the new.
- Ask him to help you value all human life and live out your beliefs regarding human life, its place and its meaning in everything you do.

» STUDY 3

GOD'S IMAGE: RELATIONSHIP

[GENESIS 2:18-25]

Marriage in our culture

THE PREVAILING ATTITUDES AND values of our culture influence us in many ways, but never more profoundly than in relation to marriage and family. As we observe our parents' marriage and grow up as a member of their family, we develop a strongly held set of values about marriage and family life. It is hard—perhaps impossible—to erase the legacy of our upbringing in this area. Furthermore, our views are usually reinforced by others in society: the friends we mix with at school, and the steady drip of images and values pumped into us by the media.

This makes it difficult for us when we approach marriage and family life as Christians. It means that if we enter marriage, we carry with us a bus load of expectations and entrenched attitudes—some of which lie just below the level of consciousness.

When we turn to the Bible for guidance about *Christian* marriage, we can be puzzled by the strange ideas we encounter, for the Bible has strong things to say about marriage. Furthermore, these strong things that the Bible says are radically different from the values of our culture.

To get in touch with what you think and feel about marriage, answer the following questions. Don't try to think up the 'right' Christian answer; answer them honestly off the top of your head.

1. What characteristics do you look for in a marriage partner?

2. Do you think sexual desire is a good reason for getting married?

3. Which of the following do you think is the major cause of marital breakdown?

   a. Marrying the wrong person/basic incompatibility

   b. Lack of communication

   c. Dissatisfying sex life

   d. Other:

Relationship in the garden

In the last study, we saw that, from the very beginning, God made man for relationship. One facet of our being made in God's image is that, like God, we are diverse and yet united, and we enjoy relationship with each other. We are male and female.

This 'relationship' theme is developed in Genesis 2, when the creation of woman is described in detail. As in Genesis 1:26-28, woman is similar to man and yet different, and the two live in a unified relationship. It is also worth noting that this pattern is established *before the Fall*. Marriage and sex are parts of God's good creation, not a consequence of the curse.

God creates the woman because there is something not good in his creation: the man is alone (Gen 2:18). God sees that mankind needs relationship. This is true in our experience as well: we humans are built for relationship—for interaction with each other. There are few human experiences more devastating than true loneliness.

As God creates a helper for Adam, we should note three things.

a) Similarity

The man needs someone who is more than an animal; he needs a helper who is "fit" for him (Gen 2:18). God meets this need by forming a helper out of the man's own body. In other words, for the relationship to be satisfactory, there must a degree of similarity between the man and woman.

b) Diversity

All the same, God does not create a second man; he creates a different, complementary being. There is similarity, but there is also diversity—Adam and Eve, not Adam and Steve.

This is important to affirm in light of some of the prevailing attitudes of our society. Many today want to eradicate any diversity between man and woman. Apart from a few minor biological differences, it is argued, there is no inherent difference between the sexes at all. They are not two different, complementary beings, but two identical beings. This does not accord with Genesis 2.

c) Unity

God intends for these two similar yet diverse beings to become a unified whole. A man will leave his father and mother, and *hold fast* to his wife, and they will become *one flesh* (Gen 2:24). This means not only setting up house together, but sexual unity. Just as they came from one flesh, so they again become one flesh in sex.

This tells us something of God's purpose for sex. Apart from the obvious reproductive function, sex is part of the bond between husband and wife; it unites them physically, but also at a more profound level. Sex is part of the glue that holds man and woman together in a unified relationship, the two of them ruling the world together as one mankind.

We also learn that the man-woman relationship has priority even over the parental bond. The fundamental unity is between husband and wife, and this unity must take priority even over parents.

Of course, this unity is not very evident in our society. With something like 40-50 per cent of marriages ending in divorce within the first 30 years (at the time of writing[1]), and many of the rest battling on in discord and anguish, the Genesis ideal of a unified mankind seems distant. This is because we live *this* side of Genesis 3, where God pronounces a curse on mankind for their rebellion against him.

The curse, as it affects marriage, is found in Genesis 3:16: "Your desire shall be for your husband, and he shall rule over you". The meaning of these strange words becomes clear when we compare them with Genesis 4:7b: God addresses Cain, saying, "And if you do not do well, sin is crouching at the door. Its *desire* is for you, but you must *rule* over it." In the Hebrew, these are the same words as in Genesis 3:16. That is, God's judgement is that the woman will desire to overthrow her husband, but he will rule over her. This is a powerful description of fallen human marriage. Instead of unity and openness, there is conflict. Each partner attempts to gain ascendancy and get their own way—the wife by the sharpness of her tongue; the husband by the strength of his biceps.

Through history, this has been the tragic reality of human relationships. Women have attacked men with their considerable emotional and verbal arsenal; men have quashed the rebellion with brute force. Today, we recognize this and keep changing partners in a futile attempt to avoid the conflict.

We need to look at what the rest of the Bible makes of these ideas. But first …

4. From these Old Testament passages, briefly write down anything you discover about marriage or how the image of marriage is used.

- Isaiah 54:5 (cf. Jer 31:31-32)

- Malachi 2:10-16

- Deuteronomy 24:1-5 (cf. Matt 19:3-9)

Read Ephesians 5:22-33.

5. Read verses 31-33 again. What is the 'profound mystery'?

6. Write down the sequence of events in the courtship and marriage between Christ and the church. (Refer to verse 27, 2 Corinthians 11:1-2 and Revelation 19:6-9.)

7. What does all this mean for earthly marriages?

THE PATTERN WE SAW EMERGE IN THE last study is also evident here. The ideal reality is established in the garden: man and woman are united in one flesh, living in relationship as the image of God. The Fall shatters this ideal state, and conflict and brokenness become a way of life in human marriage.

Then with the coming of Christ, God brings the ideal to fulfilment: Christ and his bride, the church, are united in perfect harmony and unity, thanks to the purifying work of Christ on the cross. This 'profound mystery' is the ultimate reality to which Genesis 1-2 looked forward. As with the idea of rule in the last study, the image of God is fulfilled perfectly in Christ—in this case, in the heavenly relationship between Christ and the church.

What does it mean for us? Every Christian is already engaged to be married—to Christ. This is the really important marriage, and our preparation for it is holiness. Christ has paid the bride price to win us for himself. We might even regard the gift of the Holy Spirit as an engagement ring, guaranteeing our participation in the wedding day at the end of time. In the meantime, we are to prepare ourselves for the wedding by putting on 'holiness' and 'righteous acts' as our bridal clothes. Christ wants a spotless bride without blemish; for this reason, he died for his bride to wash her clean of sin, so that he could present her to himself radiant and unspoiled.

Marriages here and now

What does all this mean for earthly marriages? Are they obsolete now that we are 'engaged' to Christ? In the past, some Christians have concluded this and have abstained from marriage altogether. (They should have read 1 Timothy 4:1-4 where Paul blasts the false teaching of those who "forbid marriage".)

Perhaps the Christians in first-century Corinth thought something like this, for in his first letter to the Corinthians, Paul addresses the issue of marriage and celibacy. If you have time, read 1 Corinthians 6:18-7:9 and note the following:

- Christians are quite free to marry or remain single; there is no sin involved in either course.
- One of the primary motivations for marriage (in fact, the only one given in this passage) is sex. If we find we cannot control our sexual desires, we should marry for "it is better to marry than to be aflame with passion" (1 Cor 7:9). This goes against the romantic grain of our culture, but that is *our* problem, not Paul's.
- We are free to marry or not, but we are *not* free about holiness. We are to flee immorality (1 Cor 6:18), for our bodies are home to God's own Spirit. Whether married or single, holiness is the crucial issue. It is far more important than marriage. In fact, we should revise the previous point to read that the motivation for marriage is holiness. If our holiness is under threat from sexual temptation, we

should marry lest our holiness be compromised.

- This all fits with what Paul says in the passages we looked at earlier. The ultimate marriage—the marriage that really counts—is our marriage to Christ, and our preparation for that marriage is holiness. The guiding principle for all our behaviour in this life, including marriage, is holiness. If we do marry, then once again, the important factor is not so much whom we marry, but the quality or holiness of the marriage. We see this in Ephesians 5:22-33, where Christ and his holy church serve as a model for the sacrificial love and submission of human marriage.

Decisions we make

There are three choices we make regarding marriage. Unfortunately there is not room here to discuss them adequately. Here are a few remarks to provoke your thinking.

a) Whether to marry

This is a genuine choice, and one to which too few Christians give serious consideration. 1 Corinthians 7 makes clear that marriage is a matter of indifference. There are distinct advantages in being single, especially in doing the Lord's work. Yet not all of us have the gift of being able to control our sexual appetites, and so we should marry.

Many modern Christians are *so* committed to the idea of marriage that they will marry an unbeliever rather than remain single. People in Bible times rarely had much choice in marriage partners, but where there was a choice (as in 1 Corinthians 7:39), they were to marry a believer. If we marry an unbeliever in our desperation to marry, we have compromised the holiness of our true marriage to Christ.

b) Whom to marry

If we have decided to marry, how should we choose a partner? Firstly, we should choose *prayerfully*, asking God to supply our need in his time. We should trust God to give us all that we need for our life in his service, including an appropriate marriage partner, if that is his will.

Secondly, we should choose *rightly*. Some aspects of our marriage choice are simple questions of right and wrong—in other words, they are questions of holiness. The person we choose must not be a blood relative, they must be free to marry (that is, they are not already married), they must be a Christian and they must be of the opposite sex. If these four criteria are met, the person is a *right* choice.

Finally, we should choose *wisely*. Given that there are a number of people who fall into the *right* category, we should exercise godly wisdom in making our choice. What sort of person would make a good husband or wife?

c) How to marry

It is a matter of freedom *whether* to marry, and there are many people who might be a right and wise choice when it comes to deciding *whom* to marry. But *how* to be married? This is the most difficult, and yet the most important, decision of all. For those of us who are married, we make this decision each day as we choose whether to follow the model of Christ and his church. Living in holiness and godliness, serving and caring for your partner, learning to lead and submit in an appropriate way—these are the daily decisions that are most difficult, but most important.

» Implications

(Choose one or more of the following to think about further or to discuss in your group.)

- If you are single, do you think *remaining* single is a serious option for you?

- Look back over the passage in Ephesians 5 and compare it with 1 Peter 3:1-7. Write down the sort of characteristics that might determine a wise choice of wife or husband.

- If you are married, look back over Ephesians 5:22-33 and 1 Peter 3:1-7. What do you find challenging about these passages regarding how you should conduct your marriage?

- How do the ideas raised in this study affect behaviour in relationships before marriage?

» Give thanks and pray

- Thank God for the goodness of marriage. Thank God for bringing about the fulfilment of marriage with Christ's work on the cross on behalf of his bride, the church.
- Pray for Christians you know who are single: ask God to give them wisdom so that they will always put on holiness when interacting with the opposite sex. Ask God to help those struggling with sexual temptation to remain pure.
- Pray for Christians you know who are married: ask God to help both husbands and wives conduct themselves in godliness and love towards one another, following the model of sacrificial love and submission outlined in Ephesians 5.

Endnote

1. Scott M Stanley, 'What really is the divorce rate?', PREP, 2003, viewed 22 March 2010: www.prepinc.com/main/Docs/what_really_div_rate.html; see also Parliament of Australia Standing Committee on Legal and Constitutional Affairs, 'To have and to hold: Strategies to strengthen marriage and relationships', Commonwealth of Australia, 1998, p. 17, viewed 22 March 2010: www.aph.gov.au/house/committee/laca/Inquiryinfam.htm

» STUDY 4

WORK AND REST

[GENESIS 2:2-3]

The working week

THE SEVEN-DAY WEEK, WITH ITS cycle of work and rest, is an entrenched part of our civilization. But why do we organize our lives like this?

For some, the pattern is work seven, rest none. Work is the sum total of their lives. They live to work, and their worth as individuals—how they feel about themselves—is inseparable from their job.

For others, work is a necessary evil that separates one weekend from the next. Monday to Wednesday, you talk about last weekend; Thursday to Friday, you plan for next weekend.

Although few realize it and fewer acknowledge it, our society has based its pattern of work and rest on Genesis 2:2-3. The fabric of western society was woven on Christian looms, and of the many things that 'post-Christian' society has inherited from its Christian past, this pattern is one.

But as we shall see, Genesis 2:2-3 is about much more than establishing some arbitrary code of work and rest; it is about the meaning of life.

The end of creation

When we reach verse 26 of Genesis 1, we have good reason to believe that the story has reached its climax. At the pinnacle of creation stands mankind—male and female, created in the image of God to rule the creation. However, man is the pinnacle, but not the end point:

> And on the seventh day God
> finished his work that he had
> done, and he rested on the
> seventh day from all his work

> that he had done. So God blessed the seventh day and made it holy, because on it God rested from all his work that he had done in creation. (Gen 2:2-3)

What happens on the last day of creation? God rests. Far from being an anticlimax, this tells us the end point—the goal to which all creation is heading: rest. As we look at the rest of the Scriptures, we discover that God's aim for man and creation is rest.

These two short verses also reveal something else about God that would be quite startling were it not so familiar: God is a worker. If God came into the world, what would he be like? For the ancient Greeks, he might have been a philosopher-king. The ancient Romans might have looked for a just and noble statesman. But how does the God of the Hebrews come into the world? As a carpenter—a worker.

God knows, then, what it is to work and rest. It is no accident that these characteristics are written into our natures. Like God, we find satisfaction in working and enjoying the fruits of our labour.

In the history of Israel, 'rest' and the 'seventh day' are recurring themes. ('Sabbath' is simply the Hebrew word for 'rest'.) Let's have a look at some key Old Testament passages.

Read Exodus 23:10-12 and Leviticus 25:8-17.

1. What were the different Sabbaths or 'rests' that the Israelites were commanded by God to observe?

2. Looking at Exodus 23:10-12, what reasons does God give for having a rest period? What sort of time is a 'Sabbath' meant to be? What are its characteristics?

Read Exodus 31:12-17.

3. What are the Sabbaths meant to signify?

4. Why do you think Sabbath-breaking was such a serious offence?

5. Now read Deuteronomy 12:7-11. Moses has led Israel to the verge of Canaan, the promised land. In what sense is 'rest' (='Sabbath') used in this passage? (Also see Psalm 95:8-11.)

6. From what you have found in the above passages, summarize how the idea of rest/Sabbath is used in the Old Testament:

-

•

•

•

Jesus and the Sabbath

As we turn to the New Testament and the Gospels, we are struck by how much conflict was generated by the issue of the Sabbath. The Pharisees levelled the charge of Sabbath-breaking at Jesus more than once, and his replies were typically forceful and enigmatic.

Stop now and read one of these conflict passages in Mark 2:23-3:6.

The Pharisees made a crucial mistake in applying the law about the rest day. We have seen so far that the Sabbath was meant to be a good day—a day for rest and refreshment, for blessing and enjoyment. The Sabbath was to be a day when Israel remembered that they were God's people, rescued out of Egypt. The Pharisees turned this day of joyful remembrance into a day of mean, nit-picking legalism. They were so worried about not working that they lost sight of what the command was really about.

However, we Christians should not cast the first stone. This same kind of legalism has characterized our attitude to the Sabbath. We are the ones who turned 'Thou shalt not work on Saturday' into 'Thou shalt not play on Sunday'. Apart from changing the day (from the seventh to the first day of the week), we have often been guilty in the past of the error of the Pharisees: we have forgotten that the Sabbath was a 'rest' day—a day of refreshment and enjoyment, a day for enjoying all the good things that God has made, and a day for remembering his mercy to us.

Jesus also did nothing for his relationship with the Pharisees in proclaiming himself 'Lord of the Sabbath' (Mark 2:28). That is, Jesus saw himself as being in charge of God's rest. (Remember, 'Sabbath' means 'rest'.) He was the one who would usher in the rest that God's people had been long awaiting—the time of blessing, the time of feasts and good times (see the passage immediately preceding this one—Mark 2:18-22). "Come to me," said Jesus, "all who labor and are heavy laden, and I will give you rest" (Matt 11:28).

To understand more about this 'rest' that Jesus was bringing, and of which he is Lord, we need to look at Hebrews 3-4. In this passage, the Old Testament idea of rest is applied to us Christians.

Read Hebrews 3:7-4:11.

7. What does it mean that the Israelites did not enter God's rest? Why were they excluded?

8. Look at Hebrews 4:6-11. The writer asserts that "there remains a Sabbath rest for the people of God" (v. 9). What does he mean?

9. What is this 'rest' that we are still to enter (cf. Rev 14:13)? How might someone be excluded from it?

Summary

Let's try to tie all these ideas together.

The last day of Creation is the day of rest. God rests and enjoys his work, and blesses that day. In the Old Testament, this pattern of creation is used as the basis of the 'rests' prescribed for Israel—resting on the seventh day, the seventh year, and the seven-times-seventh year (the fiftieth year). These rests were to be times of refreshment, blessing and generosity, when Israel remembered that they were God's people. The Sabbath rest served as a covenant sign that they were God's people.

It was also a reminder that God had rescued them out of Egypt and brought them to the promised land. This land that they inherited was referred to as 'God's rest' because in it, they received rest from oppression and their enemies, and enjoyed the bounty of a land flowing with milk and honey.

Nevertheless, in Psalm 95, David still looks for a Sabbath rest for God's people. He warns his people, who were already residents in Canaan, not to be disobedient lest they fail to enter God's rest. In other words, he was looking for some other rest—one more profound than the physical land of Canaan.

In the New Testament, Jesus ushers in this new age of rest. He comes as the Lord of the Sabbath (or rest) who gives rest to people's weary souls. Jesus has come to lead God's people to the ultimate rest—heaven. Just as Moses led Israel out of slavery, across the wilderness and into God's bountiful rest, so Jesus rescues us from our slavery to sin, leads us through this barren life and brings us to God's eternal rest.

'Rest', then, is the goal of creation. It is where creation is heading. There is more to life than work and this world; there is the world to come where man will rest with God.

What does it mean for me?

Our society doesn't have a good record when it comes to work and rest. We tend to swing between the extremes of workaholism and idleness. Perhaps our most serious failing is the importance we give to work for determining our self-worth. These days, work is the primary source of many people's satisfaction and fulfilment in life. If their job is uninteresting or unfulfilling, they feel worthless or unimportant. They are their work. Most people would describe themselves in terms of their profession: "I am a doctor"—unless, of course, they are not proud of what they do, in which case, they might say, "I am a [insert name of sports team] supporter" or "I am a father of three".

But work isn't what life, or our self-esteem, is about. Certainly, we need to work; Paul says that if someone is not prepared to work, they should not eat (2 Thess 3:6-15). But work shouldn't dominate our priorities and decisions.

In fact, if we take seriously the ideas in this study, our priorities and lifestyle should be dominated by rest, not work. For we are Christians, and Christians are people who have been rescued by Jesus from our slavery to sin and people who are looking forward to entering God's eternal rest. That is where our priorities lie. That is what we live for.

In practical terms, taking a day off each week is an expression of this commitment. It is a little symbolic taste of heaven. It reminds us that there is more to life than work. Taking a day off is a sign of my commitment to heaven, rather than to work and this world.

No particular day is specified as the Christian Sabbath in the New Testament. In fact, in the new age, we are free to consider every day alike (Rom 14:5). We should aim to take a day off each week for the refreshment of our bodies and to acknowledge that there is more to life than work. But there are no laws as to which day it should be, and what we should or shouldn't do on it.

No doubt it is appropriate to meet with God's people on that day and celebrate together what God has done for us. But there is no law about this, and there is nothing in the Bible to say that we should meet primarily on Sunday.

» Implications

(Choose one or more of the following to think about further or to discuss in your group.)

- What is your own attitude to work? Do you work too much or too little?

- What is your pattern of rest?

- How do your answers fit into the Bible's emphasis?

- How might you need to rearrange your lifestyle in order to reflect a godly pattern of work and rest?

» Give thanks and pray

- Thank God for his Sabbaths, and for Jesus, the Lord of the Sabbath. Thank God for sending Jesus to bring about eternal and permanent rest through his work on the cross.
- Ask God to transform the work culture of the world into something that glorifies him. Ask him to work in the lives of people who define themselves and derive their sense of self-worth from their work.
- Ask God to help you reflect a godly pattern of work and rest in the way you live your life.

» STUDY 5

THE DEVIL MADE ME DO IT

[GENESIS 3:1-13]

In the aftermath of failure, when we think back over why we did what we did, the question in our minds is often "Did I jump or was I pushed?" In other words, do I have anyone but myself to blame for the sin I have just committed?

This is a tough question. There are numerous 'external' factors that affect our behaviour—tiredness, what we have or have not eaten, the current state of our body chemistry/hormones, the pressures of the world and, of course, the influence of the devil. When it comes down to it, it is sometimes hard to know whether we should be blamed for a particular 'sin' or not. Is something a 'sin' if prevailing conditions made it virtually impossible for me to do otherwise? How do we untangle the web?

Making sense of all this is made all the more difficult by our capacity for justifying wrong behaviour. Our motives are hard to sort out at the best of times. Are we just avoiding responsibility for our actions by blaming external factors for our sin? But is it naive or unfair to disregard the external factors?

What, for that matter, is 'sin'?

Such are the questions that are raised when we look at Genesis 3 and its account of how sin entered our world. Let's start by having a close look at what the passage actually says.

Read Genesis 3:1–13.

1. What was the serpent's strategy?

2. What did the serpent promise would happen if Eve ate from the tree?

3. Was he right (see vv. 7, 22)?

4. What was it, precisely, that Adam and Eve ate?

5. What do you think was the essence of their sin?

6. How do Adam and Eve react to being found out?

7. In Genesis 1-2, God established a certain order in his creation. He is in authority, with man and his helper, woman, ruling over the rest of the creation. Compare this with what happens in Genesis 3. What do you notice?

8. The full consequences of their sin become apparent from verse 14 onwards, but in verses 1-13, what consequences do you see?

As sin enters the world through Adam and Eve, there are several things we should note.

a) Denial of God

The serpent begins his attack on Eve with a sneering misquotation of God's word: "Did God actually say, 'You shall not eat of any tree in the garden'?" When Eve corrects the serpent (although she also exaggerates the command; compare her words with the original in 2:16-17), the serpent goes one step further by casting direct doubt on the truth of God's words and his motives. "God is selfish", argues the serpent. "He just wants to stop you and Adam becoming like him."

Today we are often tempted to think that God's commands are not really for our good—that God is a cosmic killjoy who wants us to miss out on the good things of life. Adam and Eve lived amid abundant provision, and yet believed the lie that God's motives were impure and that he was denying them something they ought to have. Denying the basic goodness of God towards us lies at the root of much of our sin: we believe the lies—that his way is not best, that we know better and that he is out of touch with the modern world.

b) Denial of fellowship

Throughout the story, the good order that God created is reversed. Mankind is meant to rule the animal kingdom, and yet it is the animal that rises up to deceive man. Woman, who is created to be man's helper, helps him only into sin. The good relationship between man and God is shattered by their disobedience: Adam and Eve can't face God; they hide from him. They are no longer in fellowship with him.

c) Denial of responsibility

When they are found out, Adam and Eve fall over themselves trying to pass the buck. The finger points everywhere but at themselves. Adam manages to point away from himself in two directions at once: "The woman whom you gave to be with me, she gave me fruit of the tree, and I ate" (Gen 3:12). He blames the woman, as well as God for putting her there.

d) Temptation does not equal sin

The serpent was stepping outside the order of creation by prompting mankind to sin. Man was supposed to rule over the creation, but here the servant tells his master what to do. However, while the temptation did come from 'outside', man was not overwhelmed. He was not forced to sin. Eve, and then Adam, decided to follow the serpent's advice. They were responsible for their actions. God's punishment of them assumes this.

What did they eat?

Despite all that God had given them, Adam and Eve were not satisfied. But what was it that they actually did? What was it that they ate? What was the nature of their sin?

The forbidden fruit is described, somewhat cryptically, as coming from "the tree of the knowledge of good and evil" (Gen 2:17). Before looking at what this fruit was, or what it symbolized, we should note what it was *not*.

- *It was not an apple:* Despite the mythology that has grown and the widespread use of the apple as a symbol of temptation, there is no mention of apples in Genesis 3. Adam and Eve did not disobey God and subject the entire world to his judgement by eating an apple.

  It is important to affirm that the forbidden fruit was not some arbitrary choice on God's part. It is not as if he decided, on a whim, that apples were out of bounds, while oranges and watermelons were okay. Once again, we are casting God as the arbitrary killjoy.
- *It was not sex:* Advertisers like to link half-eaten apples with semi-naked women, and this reveals another popular misconception: the sin of Adam and Eve was *not* that they had sex. Sex is part of God's good creation. It is there at the end of Genesis 2, where man and woman are united by God and become "one flesh".

If the sin was not eating an apple or having sex, what was it? Clearly, it had something to do with wanting to 'know good and evil', but what does that mean? Let us note the following things:

- There were two trees in the centre of the garden—one of which was off limits to Adam and Eve: the tree of the knowledge of good and evil (Gen 2:17). It represented attributes of God —that is, eating of it would make man like God, knowing good and evil (Gen 3:22).
- Man had some concept of obedience before he ate of the tree. God's command in Genesis 2:17 assumes that man understood his obligation to obey and the consequences of disobedience. In other words, he was capable of moral choice: he understood the concepts of 'right' and 'wrong'. (This is against those who argue that man had no moral nature at all before eating of the tree.)
- Man is possessed of a certain 'naivety', which is destroyed by eating from the tree. Before eating, man was hardly aware that he was naked; it made no difference to him. But having eaten of the tree, his 'eyes were opened', he received a new level of perception, and his nakedness bothered him. He needed to cover it up. He needed to hide it from God. In the passage, this is the key illustration of man's new knowledge—that he was now aware of his nakedness and was ashamed of it. "Who told you that you were naked?" asks God (Gen 3:11).
- After eating, man has a new level of moral perception. His eyes have been opened. He understands good and evil in a way that he didn't before. The passage does not make clear the precise nature and extent of this newfound knowledge, but, at the very least, it made him 'like God' in

some sense, and it prompted him to cover his nakedness.

- Adam and Eve's rebellion is a rebellion against the order of creation. In Genesis 1-2, there is a descending chain of authority: God, man/woman and the animals. In Genesis 3, that order is overturned. The rebellion starts with the animal who prompts woman, and then man, to usurp the place of God.
- The essence of their sin is *a desire to become like God*. They are not satisfied with what God has given them, plentiful as that provision is; they want to know what God knows. Their sin is not simply breaking some arbitrary test of obedience; they are trying to take the place of God. They reject God's authority and his knowledge of what is good and best for them. In other words, their sin is much more than a momentary lapse of obedience; it is an act of revolution.

  This is important to grasp because it runs counter to the beliefs of most people in our society. Most people believe that sin is breaking rules. They believe that for his own mainly sadistic reasons, God has established certain rules and that we sin when we break them. Genesis 3 teaches us that sin is much more than breaking a rule like a parking offence; sin is revolution: it is denying the way God has made things, rejecting his authority and trying to put ourselves in the place of God.

We will look at the consequences of Adam and Eve's rebellion in the next study; suffice to say at this stage that God reinforces the natural consequences of their sin. Man upset the order of creation, and now he must live with the consequences: conflict between man and woman, painful childbirth, and an environment that is hostile and that yields crops reluctantly.

Adam and Eve and us

As we think about how these ideas affect us today, we need to bear in mind the following.

a) We are all involved

Adam's sin is our sin. The important passage to look at is Romans 5:12-21. Here, Paul compares the sin of Adam with Christ's gift of salvation. Just as through one man, sin and death came to all men, so through the one man, Jesus Christ, justification and life comes to all men. There is a solidarity between Adam and all of us. His sin affected his descendants. We are born into a family and a world already deeply committed to sin, and from the very youngest age, our own predisposition is also to rebel against authority and do things our own way.

The Bible teaches that all men everywhere rebel against God. In this sense, we inherit a nature that is rebellious against God—a nature that is deeply flawed and ultimately self-centred. This is true in our own experience. Other philosophies deny this, asserting that man is basically good and capable of improving his lot. The Bible, and any sane assessment of history, show otherwise—that man's nature is deeply and inherently flawed—that we are selfish and want no-one, least of all God, to tell us what to do.

b) We are each responsible

While we are naturally disposed to sin, the Bible also makes clear that we each choose, wilfully and deliberately, to rebel against God: "just as sin came into the world through one man, and death through sin, and so death spread to all men because all sinned …" (Rom 5:12). Even in Romans 5, where Paul emphasizes that condemnation came to all men through the sin of Adam, the responsibility that each of us has for our sin also peeps through. Death came to all men because all sinned (v. 12).

This tension between our choice and the factors that determine that choice is found everywhere in life. We are conditioned and determined by a multitude of forces: upbringing, environment, body chemistry, government decisions, and so on. Yet our will is never completely subjected to these factors. We still deliberately choose, and are thus accountable for our actions.

c) We still fall for the devil's deceit

The serpent persuaded Eve that God's word was not true and that his motives were impure. Eve believed that she ought to give the forbidden fruit a try. We also swallow this lie about God. We believe that he doesn't know best and that our way is better than his way. We believe the lie that we will be happier if we sin. Paul uses Eve as an example to warn the Corinthians in the eleventh chapter of his second letter to them: "But I am afraid that as the serpent deceived Eve by his cunning, your thoughts will be led astray from a sincere and pure devotion to Christ." (2 Cor 11:3).

» Implications

- Think for a moment, and write down the areas in which you are tempted to think that God does not know what is best. In what areas are you rebelling against his good rule?

» Give thanks and pray

- Confess your sins to God and ask him for his forgiveness.
- Thank and praise God for Jesus who came to deal with our sin once and for all.
- Ask God to help you trust him—trust that his way is best and that he always knows what's good for you. Ask him to help you to be obedient to his will.

» STUDY 6

THE CURSE

[GENESIS 3]

Life is a strange mix

I WAS LISTENING TO THE RADIO NOT so long ago when they played the remix of Louis Armstrong's gravelly classic 'What a wonderful world'. Do you know it? As Louis looks around him and sees the trees of green, the red roses, the colours of the rainbow, the babies crying and the friends greeting each other, he thinks to himself, "What a wonderful world". And if we're feeling a bit sentimental, we nod and think, "Yes, it *is* a wonderful world".

However, after the song finished, it was time for the hourly news. It contained the usual litany of destruction, death, conflict and bad news. So much for the wonderful world!

This often bizarre mixture of good and evil touches us almost every day. There is much that is beautiful, noble, loving and admirable. But there seems an equal (if not greater) quantity of distrust, disaster, chaos and brokenness.

Of course, it touches us most severely when the evil is personal and immediate. When our child dies of cancer, it is hard to believe that God is either good or in control. How could he be? It's just not right. It's not fair. We shake our heads, because we know, at a deeper level, that he is both good and in control. Life is a strange mix.

As we look in this study at the 'curse' of Genesis 3, and at what the rest of the Bible makes of it, we'll come some way to understanding why life is such a strange mix, and what God plans to do about it.

Read Genesis 3.

1. What are the curses against:
   - the serpent?
   - the woman?
   - the man?

An alternative government

What sort of world did Adam and Eve face outside the garden of Eden? Now that they had become like God, knowing good and evil, what sort of world would they shape for themselves? They had rejected the rule of God and so, presumably, were free to be their own masters, to make their own mistakes, to forge their own just society.

If only this were true.

The truth is, of course, that in rejecting God, man did not free himself to be his own master. Far from it; he simply replaced the one true master (God) with another set of masters. The rest of the Bible spells out the nature of these new rulers and the type of dominion they enjoy over mankind.

a) Deceit

The cause of man's undoing was a lie, and from that point on, we have been children of the father of lies (Gen 3:1-5; John 8:42-47; 2 Cor 11:3). Our world is built on lies, starting with the Big Lie that God is not God and that we don't need to obey him. While we know that God is there and should be honoured, we choose to suppress this knowledge and believe the lie (Rom 1:18ff).

In practical terms, the reign of deceit affects us every day, for everyone we meet is a liar. We all do it—we all tell lies—even though we applaud the principle of honesty. Mankind is incapable of being consistently truthful.

b) Darkness

However, our captivity goes further. We are not simply under the rule of an impersonal principle called 'deceit'; the Bible makes it quite clear that, having rejected God's rule, we have placed ourselves in the power of malignant forces of darkness. We don't need to 'sell our souls to the devil', like Faust; the devil already owns them.

This is taught in numerous places in the New Testament. Jesus describes those who do not believe his words as children of the devil (John 8:43-44). Paul is also quite aware of the influence of these spiritual powers. These are the powers that have blinded the minds of unbelievers so that they cannot see the light of Christ (2 Cor 4:4). This is the domain from which Christ rescues (Col 1:13). And these are forces against which we still struggle as Christians (Eph 6:12).

As sophisticated 21st-century people, we may find all this talk of devils and evil powers a little hard to believe. We like to think that we are our own masters. This is, perhaps, the greatest deceit of all.

c) Death

Whenever we confront death, we are horrified at how stark and simple it is—and yet, how unnatural. When someone dies, we think, "No, this should not be! It is not right." And this is a right perception, for death was not always the universal experience of mankind.

Death is a consequence of our rejection of God. God's punishment, you will remember, is to banish man from the garden and bar the way to the tree of life. Man cuts himself off from God, the source of all life, and so dies. In rejecting God, we reject life. At a number of points, the Bible traces the entry of death into the world back to Adam. With the sin of Adam and God's enforcement of the consequences, we come under the grim reign of death (Rom 5:12-21, 6:23; 1 Cor 15:21).

d) Decay

God's curse extends to the very creation itself. The ground is cursed and no longer yields its produce easily. The world in which we live is a fallen place. It too has a new master: decay.

Romans 8:18-25 is an important passage on this point, and we will study it in more detail in a moment. The creation, Paul says, has been subjected to frustration; it has been placed in "bondage to corruption" (Rom 8:21). We should not be surprised, then, that terrible things happen in the world. We should expect them because the world is groaning and creaking, waiting to be freed from its broken state.

Getting it right

God has given us over to the consequences of our rebellion. His punishment or curse is that we suffer the tragic results of our sin: having rejected his rule, we find ourselves trapped under the fourfold regime of deceit, darkness, death and decay.

Even so, God does not let the world degenerate entirely; we still see his hand at work. He still sends the rain on the just and the unjust alike, and we still catch glimpses of the world as good and beautiful.

Will it always be this way? Will life always be a strange mix? What is God doing about it? To answer our questions, we need to look at the New Testament.

Read 1 Corinthians 15:20-28, 45-49.

2. In what ways are Adam and Christ alike?

3. In what ways are they different?

Read Romans 8:18-25.

4. How does Paul describe the current state of the world?

5. When and how will this be changed?

6. What, then, is to be our attitude to suffering?

» Implications

(Choose one or more of the following to think about further or to discuss in your group.)

- Where have you experienced the rule of evil? In what areas are you tempted to think that God has been unfair to you?

- How should we react when our lives are touched by tragedy or suffering?

- How will the evil and suffering in the world be resolved?

- "Our best efforts at alleviating the suffering of the world are little better than bandaids." Do you agree with this statement? Why? Why not?

- What are you doing while you wait for the liberation of the world?

» Give thanks and pray

- Thank God for his goodness in freeing us from deceit, darkness, death and decay by Jesus' life, death and resurrection.
- Praise God for the hope of heaven and the end of suffering.
- Ask God to help you to view tragedy and suffering the way he does. Ask him to help you endure these things by keeping your trust firmly in him.

» STUDY 7

THE GOD I DON'T BELIEVE IN

[GENESIS 6–9]

CHRISTIANS ARE OFTEN ACCUSED of creating God in our own image. It is said that we feel a need for security, hope, certainty or love, and construct a divine figure to fill those needs. God is born of necessity, or so it is argued.

The irony in this accusation is that *non*-Christians are much more prone to make God in their image. If one rejects the revealed God of the Bible and theorizes about the nature of a possible divine being, the result will be a deity reflecting human concerns and values. You see this when people use phrases like "I like to think of God as …" or "The God I believe in wouldn't …" In the end, their god is a slightly magnified version of themselves: 'He'/'She' hates what they hate, and is tolerant of what they tolerate.

It is easy for Christians to do the same. When we find some aspect of God's character unpalatable, it is tempting to reinterpret that section of the Bible, or gloss over it, or assign it to the cultural rubbish bin.

One aspect of God's character that we sometimes find hard to swallow and that non-Christians never include in their construction of God is his anger. A Spanish priest, Juan Arias, has written a book called *The God I Don't Believe In*, in which he debunks some modern myths about God. Many of the things he says are quite true and helpful, but it is interesting to read his comments on the anger of God.

> No, I shall never believe in:
> the God who catches man by
> surprise in a sin of
> weakness …

the God who loves pain …
the God who makes himself
feared …
the God incapable of smiling at
many of man's awkward
mistakes,
the God who "plays at"
condemning
the God who "sends" people
to hell,
the God who always demands 100
percent in examinations …
the God who says "You will pay
for that!" …
the God who prefers purity
to love …[1]

Arias makes the mistake of equating God's anger with its human counterpart. Human anger is often exactly like Arias's description—vindictive, impulsive and high-handed. But God's anger is very different: God's anger is slow and righteous. It is not the opposite of love—far from it; God's wrath is the very expression of his love.

What is the opposite of love? Every parent knows that the answer to that question is indifference. Discipline and punishment are part of loving our children. It might not be pleasant or desirable, but we know that if we are to care for our children, we must show them that their behaviour matters to us. We must demonstrate that we care so much about what they do, we are prepared to inflict punishment—an action that is painful for both parent and child. The parent who treats a disobedient child with indifference transmits a powerful message to the child: "I do not care".

Deterioration

The opening verses of Genesis 6 indicate that God had much to be angry about. In Genesis 1, "God saw everything that he had made, and behold, it was very good" (Gen 1:31), but now he sees a very different picture: "The LORD saw that the wickedness of man was great in the earth, and that every intention of the thoughts of his heart was only evil continually" (Gen 6:5).

The situation had deteriorated. Mankind was a blot on the landscape, and God was grieved by it. He cared about his world—he loved his world. And when he looked at it and saw it inhabited with evil, his heart was filled with pain (see Gen 6:5-6).

God determines to wipe out mankind. This is not done in a fit of rage or pique; it is his slow and deliberate response to the evil he sees. As we might expect from God, he does not confront evil with indifference or half-measures; his response is judgement mixed with salvation.

Read Genesis 6:11-9:17.

Read Genesis 6:11-8:14 to remind yourself of the details of the narrative. Now read Genesis 8:15-9:17.

1. What is Noah's response as he comes safely out of the ark?

2. Has mankind's heart been changed by the Flood?

3. What is God's covenant with Noah, and what is to be its sign?

4. To what extent have Lamech's words in Genesis 5:29 been fulfilled?

Read Genesis 9:18-29.

5. Who gets cursed? Why?

What does it all mean?

THE STORY OF NOAH AND THE FLOOD is a Sunday School favourite, and it is difficult for us to escape this mindset when we read it as adults. We tend to be very interested in the details and in answering our own questions about the narrative. There are plenty that spring to mind:

- Who were the Nephilim and the sons of God (Gen 6:1-4)?
- Did the Flood really cover the whole world or just the 'world' of the author (i.e. Mesopotamia)?
- Was mankind allowed to eat meat before this (Gen 9:1-3)?
- Is the ground still cursed in the same way that it was before the Flood (Gen 8:21)?

These questions are difficult to answer, but none of them gives us any real clue to the overall meaning of the Flood story. One important clue is found in an earlier passage in Genesis when God curses the serpent:

> "I will put enmity between you
> and the woman,
> and between your offspring and
> her offspring;
> he shall bruise your head,
> and you shall bruise his heel."
> (Gen 3:15)

God promises that Eve's offspring and the serpent's will continue to be enemies. The expectation is raised: will there be a son of Eve who might finally defeat the evil of the serpent? As the generations come and go, we look for this saviour—this one who will reverse the effects of the curse. At first, it seems like Noah might be the one.

He is distinguished by his righteous behaviour and his obedience to God's commands. Noah takes God at his word. He is told, without there being any visible evidence, that the world will be deluged and that he needs to build an ark. He obeys. It is no easy thing, and yet he does it.

After the Flood, his response is also godly: he offers pleasing sacrifices to God in thanksgiving for the salvation of his family. And when in Genesis 8:21, God says in his heart that he will never again curse the ground or destroy the world in the way he has, the prediction of Lamech in Genesis 5:29 is fulfilled—at least to an extent. Noah does provide comfort and salvation for mankind.

Moreover, God makes a covenant with the whole world through Noah. Noah is the representative man whose obedience and faith give mankind a future. Noah is an impressive figure.

All the same, he is not the saviour implicitly hoped for in Genesis 3. He plants a vineyard, gets drunk on his own wine and lies around naked. Evil triumphs over even the mighty Noah.

The Flood and us

Noah and the Flood are not mentioned much in the rest of the Bible. But when they are, it is often as a symbol of judgement. In 2 Peter 3, for example, we read:

> … knowing this first of all, that scoffers will come in the last days with scoffing, following their own sinful desires. They will say, "Where is the promise of his coming? For ever since the fathers fell asleep, all things are continuing as they were from the beginning of creation." For they deliberately overlook this fact, that the heavens existed long ago, and the earth was formed out of water and through water by the word of God, and that by means of these the world that then existed was deluged with water and perished. But by the same word the heavens and earth that now exist are stored up for fire, being kept until the day of judgment and destruction of the ungodly. (2 Pet 3:3-7)

The Flood shows us that God knows how to *judge*. It reveals God's character. He is grieved by human wickedness to the extent that he is prepared to destroy his own creation.

Our world needs to know about the judgement of God. As our society becomes increasingly remote from its Christian foundations, the concept of God being capable of anger or judgement is receding. Recent surveys suggest that outside Christian circles, virtually no Australian believes that God will judge. This presents us with a challenge.

We must communicate God's holy anger and judgement to our contemporaries. Without an understanding of God's anger, the cross of Christ becomes meaningless. Our gospel is that Jesus bore God's righteous anger in our place. If our society does not believe in God's anger, how are we to explain the cross?

There is also a subtle pressure for Christians to dump the idea of God's judgement. We are out of step with our contemporaries on this issue, and we can be made to feel foolish and old-fashioned. However, we need to treat God as *God*. We cannot pigeonhole him, or tell him what he is like; we must deal with him as he is. And the Flood narrative makes it quite clear that he is a God of judgement and destruction, as well as salvation.

However, the story of the Flood also shows us that God knows how to *save*. In fact, God's response to human wickedness in Noah's day is characteristic of his dealings with his people throughout history. He judges and destroys, yet he also graciously saves. In the midst of judgement, God works salvation. This description could apply just as well to the cross of Christ.

In many ways, Noah is a model for us: he heard God's warning about the coming judgement and made preparations; he took God at his word, put his trust in him, and was saved with his whole family. We would do well to imitate him.

» Implications

(Choose one or more of the following to think about further or to discuss in your group.)

- Do you take God's judgement seriously? If not, why not?

- Do you feel embarrassed about telling your friends about a God who is a judge?

- What effect do you think a knowledge of the judgement of God might have on our lives?

» Give thanks and pray

- Thank God for the justness and holiness of his judgement.
- Thank God for providing the true saviour who reverses the curse of the Fall: Jesus Christ, God's one and only Son.
- Ask God to help you emulate Noah's righteous behaviour in taking God at his word and trusting in him.
- Ask God to give you the wisdom to speak about God's judgement truthfully and winsomely with unbelievers.

Endnote

1. Juan Arias, *The God I Don't Believe In*, Abbey Press, St Meinrad, 1973, pp. 196-99.

» STUDY 8

THE TOWER OF BABEL

[GENESIS 11:1-9]

I have a dream

The Reverend Martin Luther King Jr was assassinated back in 1968, but since then, his famous 'I have a dream' speech is still looked back upon as a rallying cry for all who long for a better world.

The wistful expectation that mankind is on the verge of fulfilling this dream never fades, and today, the expectation is as strong as ever. The strands of progress seem to be tying together: there is a growing acknowledgement (even by politicians) that we need to protect the environment; totalitarian communism has collapsed in eastern Europe; and the technological leaps forward of the past 30 years promise solutions to some of our most serious problems. This irresistible mix of positive forces is seen by many to indicate a change for the better—a movement towards peace, cooperation and justice.

The ubiquitous Dr David Suzuki (his name means 'Messiah' to some and simply 'motorbike' to others) proclaims a message of global doom if we do not mend our ways (and our worn-out boots and clothing). He looks forward to a future in which man, having mastered his situation and made sensible plans, will forge a satisfying and sustainable existence for himself on our fragile planet.

For many modern idealists, this glorious future (and it always seems to be in the future) will spring from a marriage between cooperation and technology. If we could only work *together* to harness the knowledge and skills we possess, then surely no problem would be insurmountable. If we would only stop fighting each other, we could solve our problems.

As the global village becomes smaller and more intertwined, the possibility of a united, progressive world where wealth is distributed equitably and peace reigns somehow seems nearer. Given the astonishing technological advances of our generation, many believe that it is only a matter of time before we will master our environment. Through research and scientific enquiry, a new and better age beckons. Or so it is argued.

I have a nightmare

For the moment, at least, the dream remains a dream. Martin Luther King Jr was a great man, and he spearheaded a movement that achieved a measure of racial reform in the United States. But America's racial problems are by no means solved, and a swag of other social problems have since arisen.

Technology continues to advance, but to what end? The high-powered rifle that took Martin Luther King Jr's life was a product of the same technological society that produced vaccines to combat disease and sophisticated agricultural techniques to boost food production.

The dream of a better world built on cooperation and technology easily becomes a nightmare—a nightmare where technology booms in a moral vacuum. In the absence of values, sophisticated technology is a frightening tool. It gives us the capacity to do evil in a multitude of new ways.

The controversy surrounding the use of biomedical technology is just one example of a field in which technology has outstripped ethics. If we *can* do something, does that mean we *should* do it? It seems that some in the scientific community would answer 'Yes' to this question.

When our alarming technological advances are combined with a degree of unity, the nightmare only intensifies. History records the brutal power of collective human effort combined with technology. The great world empires (from Greece and Rome onwards) have all been built on this foundation.

What is the Bible's attitude to technology? What hope does it hold for a better world? Not surprisingly, given the period in which it was written, the Bible does not have a lot to say about technological advances and the global village. But one passage worth musing on is the intriguing story of the tower of Babel.

Read Genesis 11:1-9.

1. What reasons did the children of man have for building the city?

2. Who were they trying to impress? Among whom were they trying to "make a name" for themselves (v. 4)?

3. Do you think the children of man's actions were similar in any way to those of Adam and Eve? If so, how were they similar?

4. What was God's reaction to the plan?

A biblical theme

ALTHOUGH THIS PASSAGE IS NOT quoted directly in the rest of the Bible, its thinking is reflected in a number of places. Mankind is always seen as divided by God's purpose and will. God sets the various places for man to live (Deut 32:8), and in doing so, prompts him to reach out for God (Acts 17:26-27). God divides mankind so that we will look to him, rather than to our own united, technological power.

This division is part of the 'frustration' of the creation spoken of in Romans 8. As part of his judgement against us and to encourage us to seek him, God continues to divide mankind. It is the character of our world.

The idealist does not like this. He longs for a world of peace, where all war and division is done away with and where mankind can live in brotherhood. The Bible's view is that in this world, it will not happen. Division is the norm. It is part of God's purposes. He has 'given us over' to the consequences of our rebellion against him, and those consequences are not good (Rom 1:18-32).

The Bible also says that the arrogance of man at the tower of Babel is an ongoing feature of his nature. Man has continued to strive to be god in the world—to band together and control his environment. Nebuchadnezzar's 90-foot image of gold in Babylon was a repeat of Babel (Daniel 3; cf. Daniel 4); he wanted to unite his kingdom under the worship of this image, but God humiliated him.

Ultimately, any human system that attempts to unite mankind to rule the world is futile, regardless of whether it springs from the megalomania of Adolph Hitler or the noble aspirations of the United Nations.

Realistic idealists

The tower of Babel is the story of man wanting to be like God. Through collective effort and the application of technology, the men on the Plain of Shinar (= Babylon) sought to reach the heavens; they wanted to be gods of their own situation.

This, of course, is half true (like all good lies). We are meant to rule the world (Gen 1:26-28), but not in the place of God. Mankind is to have dominion over the earth, but as God's agents, not his rivals.

The tower of Babel changes our attitude to technology and society. Technology is not bad in itself, but its uses can be. When man strives to be god in his world by the application of technology, he acts in defiance of his maker and is destined to fail.

Society will always be divided. We must not expect it to be otherwise. To think that we will one day be able to live on this earth in unity and peace is not a Christian way of thinking. Like Abraham, we are looking forward to a better city, "the city that has foundations, whose designer and builder is God" (Heb 11:10).

The tower of Babel urges us to become

realistic idealists. We may still long for peace, unity and harmony, but we know that it will never happen this side of eternity. It will only happen when God takes action. It will happen spiritually as God regenerates his people, and it will happen physically at the end of the age. We still have our ideals, but they are tempered with reality.

We cannot conclude without noting that there is one particular form of action that *will* make a difference: the proclamation of the kingdom of God. Through this activity (in which we partner God), people are genuinely transformed. A new social order is created. People who have been changed by the gospel have both a motive and a power for pursuing the dream.

But they dream with their eyes open.

» Implications

(Choose one or more of the following to think about further or to discuss in your group.)

- How do you think the story of the tower of Babel should affect our attitude towards:
    - technology?
    - the improvement of society?
- Is all this a charter for non-involvement? Does this view of the world give rise to a kind of pessimism, in which we shrug our shoulders in the face of disunity, disease and injustice, and do nothing? If not, why not?

- What can we do? What is our contribution?

» Give thanks and pray

- Confess the times when you have used technology to replace God. Thank God for the good things in the world that technology brings. Ask him to help you view technology rightly—as a tool to be wielded under his lordship.
- Ask God to help you to be a realistic idealist.
- Thank God for allowing you to be his fellow worker in the work of the proclamation of his kingdom. Ask him to give you opportunities to spread the gospel.

» STUDY 9

IN SEARCH OF THE SAVIOUR

[GENESIS 5, 9-11]

TRACING OUR ROOTS IS ONE WAY of understanding who we are—personally and socially. It has become very fashionable for middle-class people to research their family tree and locate when and how their ancestors migrated to, say, Australia, where they came from and whether they arrived at Her Majesty's pleasure.

Even so, compiling our genealogies usually does little to alter the course of our lives. The information is not crucial to us, and most do it simply out of curiosity.

We are a little puzzled, then, upon reading the genealogies in Genesis 5, 9, 10 and 11. They seem to serve no useful purpose, and if we were compiling a condensed version of the Bible, these are chapters we would no doubt leave out. Why are they there? What was the author of Genesis trying to achieve?

To add to our confusion, the rest of the Bible regards these genealogies, and others like them, as significant. Two of the Gospel writers, Matthew and Luke, see fit to include the genealogy of Jesus in their gospel message. For them, genealogies were not something to skim over, but an important pointer to the identity of Jesus. But we are skipping ahead of ourselves.

First, let us take a quick look at the chapters in Genesis.

Read Genesis 5.

1. This list of Adam's descendants is highly patterned. Write down the pattern of words used for each generation, leaving blanks for the details that change with each generation.

2. The pattern is broken on a couple of occasions. Who are the people involved? Can you detect any significance in why the verses concerning these people are different?

Read Genesis 9:18-29.

3. What was the long-term consequence of this incident?

Read Genesis 11:10-32.

4. Towards what person or event is this genealogy leading?

The search

As we read these strange chapters, we search for some significance—some thread of continuity. However, the key to understanding them lies not in our search for a meaning, but in their search. In these chapters, the author is searching for something—or more precisely, someone.

The search starts in Genesis 3. In many ways, Genesis 1-3 is a self-contained unit. It sets out to explain why the world is the way it is—how it came to exist and why it is in such a mess. It does this concisely and powerfully, and, in one sense, we don't need to read any further. The Bible could well stop at the end of Genesis 3, and the story would make complete sense.

Except, that is, for Genesis 3:15, where God addresses the serpent:

> I will put enmity between you
> and the woman,
> and between your offspring and
> her offspring;
> he shall bruise your head,
> and you shall bruise his heel.

Genesis 3:15 gives us hope that the curse may one day be reversed. It promises that the woman's offspring and the serpent will continue to be at odds, with the implicit hope that one day the serpent might finally be defeated.

At the end of Genesis 3, we are left wondering about this serpent conflict. Who will come next to battle against the serpent? Will he defeat sin and evil?

It is not surprising that chapter 4 opens with Eve giving birth to a man—an offspring. Will he be the one?

Cain is not the one. Sin crouches at his door, and he does not crush it. He yields to it, and kills his brother, Abel. As Cain's line unfolds, concluding with the appalling Lamech, it becomes clear that we will have to look elsewhere for the serpent-bruiser.

Sure enough, Adam has another son: Seth. Is Seth the one? All he does is have children, who have children, who have children. On it goes, generation after generation, and there is still no offspring worthy to defeat the serpent.

There is some hope with Enoch who, it is said, "walked with God" (Gen 5:22). But he mysteriously disappears from the scene before he does very much—apart, that is, from having children.

The next interruption in the repetitive pattern of birth and death is Noah. Will he be the one? At first, it seems like he might be. His name means 'comfort', and his father, Lamech, seems certain that Noah will "bring us relief from our work and from the painful toil of our hands" (Gen 5:29). Perhaps Noah will crush the serpent and reverse the effects of the curse.

Noah is certainly the means by which God saves mankind from the destruction of the Flood, but he still fails to be the Satan-crusher. He gets drunk and lies around naked, causing the downfall of one his sons, Ham. From this episode, it becomes apparent that the 'right' family line will be

Shem's. His line will be blessed.

In chapter 11, we continue the search down through Shem's descendants, until we reach Abram, that giant of the Old Testament. Up to this point, the entire history of the world has been related in eleven chapters. Now one man, Abram, will be the focus of the next 13 chapters.

God declares Abram to be the father of his man: Abram will be the father of a great nation, and through it, God will bless all the nations of the earth (Gen 12:1-3). In fact, Abram's name means 'father'. There is only one problem: he has no children. In chapter 17, God changes his name to 'Abraham', which means 'father of many', but still he has no children. Finally, the child of the promise is born: Isaac (Gen 21:1-7). Will he be the one? Abraham almost kills Isaac at God's command (Genesis 22)—and in the light of this search, we see the significance of that incident. But Isaac does not turn out to be the saviour. All he does is … have children.

Down through the generations of Israel the search continues. There are heroes and saviours, and people like David, with whom God has a special relationship. But no-one rises to slay the serpent and destroy his evil work.

No-one, that is, until a man is born in the city of David—a man who can trace his ancestry through his father Joseph back to David, and from David back to Jacob, Abraham, Noah, Seth, Adam and God.

5. Look up the following verses and note how they reveal Jesus as the fulfilment of Genesis 3:15.

- Luke 3:23-38 (note what follows this genealogy in 4:1ff)

- Luke 10:17-24

- John 12:31-33

- Romans 16:20

- Colossians 2:15

- Hebrews 2:14

- 1 John 3:8b

What's the hold-up?

Throughout his earthly ministry, Jesus was in conflict with Satan, culminating in the cross. At Calvary, Satan struck and killed Jesus, but in so doing, was himself crushed and defeated. Jesus came to destroy the rule of Satan, and he achieved this through his death and resurrection.

This leaves us with an obvious question: if the serpent was finally defeated at the cross, why does evil continue in our world? Why are the effects of the curse still with us? What's the hold-up?

All of these questions are answered by the 'already/not yet' theme that runs through the New Testament. Jesus has already won the victory. Satan has been defeated. He has fallen like lightning from the sky. The means by which he accused us and held us in his power have been destroyed. His head has been crushed. The victory is *already* won.

However, the final consummation of the victory is still to come. We still await the mopping up of the remaining pockets of resistance. The decisive battle has been won, but its full expression in our world has *not yet* arrived.

Our present existence is therefore one of tension—tension between the *already* and the *not yet*. Satan still prowls around like a roaring lion, seeking someone to devour (1 Pet 5:8), and yet we need only resist him and he will flee (Jas 4:7).

Why has God delayed things this way? To give time for repentance—to give time for his people to spread the good news about Jesus' victory (2 Pet 3:9).

Genesis and us

Perhaps now we can begin to see the significance of the strange genealogies of Genesis. They are part of the record of God's grand design to save the world through a man—the man, Jesus Christ.

God's design may have focused on only one tribe, and one family in that tribe, but through that one family, he brought salvation to every nation. God was concerned for the whole of his cursed world, and that begs the question: are we concerned for the whole world?

» Implications

(Choose one or more of the following to think about further or to discuss in your group.)

- If some outside person were to assess your life, would they conclude that you were waiting for a better world, or that you were quite happy with this one?

- Kings, princes and prophets all longed to know what we now know—that Jesus is the long-awaited saviour (1 Pet 1:10-12). What effect does that knowledge have on our lives?

- How are you seeking to share the news of Jesus' victory
    - at work/school/university?
    - with friends?
    - with family?

» Give thanks and pray

- Thank God for working throughout history to bring about his plan of salvation in the life, death and resurrection of the Lord Jesus Christ.
- Thank God for Jesus, the ultimate serpent-bruiser, who defeated death, the devil and the devil's minions to bring us eternal life.
- Ask God to give you patience as you wait for the final consummation of Jesus' victory. As you wait, ask him to help you to live in such a way that glorifies him.
- Ask God to give you a heart like Jesus' that longs for the salvation of the world. Ask him to give you opportunities to speak about him to your non-Christian friends and family.

Feedback on this resource We really appreciate getting feedback about our resources—not just suggestions for how to improve them, but also positive feedback and ways they can be used. We especially love to hear that the resources may have helped someone in their Christian growth.

You can send feedback to us via the 'Feedback' menu in our online store, or write to us at PO Box 225, Kingsford NSW 2032, Australia.

Other Interactive and Topical Bible Studies from Matthias Media

Our Interactive Bible Studies (IBS) and Topical Bible Studies (TBS) are a valuable resource to help you keep feeding from God's word. The IBS series works through passages and books of the Bible; the TBS series pulls together the Bible's teaching on topics such as money or prayer. As at May 2010, the series contains the following titles:

Beyond Eden
GENESIS 1-11
Authors: Phillip Jensen and Tony Payne, 9 studies

Out of Darkness
EXODUS 1-18
Author: Andrew Reid, 8 studies

The Shadow of Glory
EXODUS 19-40
Author: Andrew Reid, 7 studies

The One and Only
DEUTERONOMY
Author: Bryson Smith, 8 studies

The Good, the Bad and the Ugly
JUDGES
Author: Mark Baddeley, 10 studies

Famine and Fortune
RUTH
Authors: Barry Webb and David Höhne, 4 studies

Renovator's Dream
NEHEMIAH
Authors: Phil Campbell and Greg Clarke, 7 studies

The Eye of the Storm
JOB
Author: Bryson Smith, 6 studies

The Search for Meaning
ECCLESIASTES
Author: Tim McMahon, 9 studies

Two Cities
ISAIAH
Authors: Andrew Reid and Karen Morris, 9 studies

Kingdom of Dreams
DANIEL
Authors: Andrew Reid and Karen Morris, 9 studies

Burning Desire
OBADIAH AND MALACHI
Authors: Phillip Jensen and Richard Pulley, 6 studies

Warning Signs
JONAH
Author: Andrew Reid, 6 studies

On That Day
ZECHARIAH
Author: Tim McMahon, 8 studies

Full of Promise
THE BIG PICTURE OF THE O.T.
Authors: Phil Campbell and Bryson Smith, 8 studies

The Good Living Guide
MATTHEW 5:1-12
Authors: Phillip Jensen and Tony Payne, 9 studies

News of the Hour
MARK
Authors: Peter Bolt and Tony Payne, 10 studies

Proclaiming the Risen Lord
LUKE 24-ACTS 2
Author: Peter Bolt, 6 studies

Mission Unstoppable
ACTS
Author: Bryson Smith, 10 studies

The Free Gift of Life
ROMANS 1-5
Author: Gordon Cheng, 8 studies

The Free Gift of Sonship
ROMANS 6-11
Author: Gordon Cheng, 8 studies

The Freedom of Christian Living
ROMANS 12-16
Author: Gordon Cheng, 7 studies

Free for All
GALATIANS
Authors: Phillip Jensen and Kel Richards, 8 studies

Walk this Way
EPHESIANS
Author: Bryson Smith, 8 studies

Partners for Life
PHILIPPIANS
Author: Tim Thorburn, 8 studies

The Complete Christian
COLOSSIANS
Authors: Phillip Jensen and Tony Payne, 8 studies

To the Householder
1 TIMOTHY
Authors: Phillip Jensen and Greg Clarke, 9 studies

Run the Race
2 TIMOTHY
Author: Bryson Smith, 6 studies

The Path to Godliness
TITUS
Authors: Phillip Jensen and Tony Payne, 7 studies

From Shadow to Reality
HEBREWS
Author: Joshua Ng, 10 studies

The Implanted Word
JAMES
Authors: Phillip Jensen and Kirsten Birkett, 8 studies

Homeward Bound
1 PETER
Authors: Phillip Jensen and Tony Payne, 10 studies

All You Need to Know
2 PETER
Author: Bryson Smith, 6 studies

The Vision Statement
REVELATION
Author: Greg Clarke, 9 studies

Bold I Approach
PRAYER
Author: Tony Payne, 6 studies

Cash Values
MONEY
Author: Tony Payne, 5 studies

Sing for Joy
SINGING IN CHURCH
Author: Nathan Lovell, 6 studies

The Blueprint
DOCTRINE
Authors: Phillip Jensen and Tony Payne, 9 studies

Woman of God
THE BIBLE ON WOMEN
Author: Terry Blowes, 8 studies

Also from Matthias Media

Genesis 1-11 on MP3 CD

For those who would like further input on Genesis 1-11, a set of talks is available which expounds the passages looked at in *Beyond Eden*. These sermons provide additional insights and ideas, and tie the material together in a way that is possible in a sermon, but not in a group Bible study.

These nine talks by Phillip Jensen are an ideal accompaniment to the studies in *Beyond Eden*, especially for group leaders who want to do some additional preparation.

FOR MORE INFORMATION OR TO ORDER CONTACT:

Matthias Media
Telephone: +61-2-9663-1478
Facsimile: +61-2-9663-3265
Email: info@matthiasmedia.com.au
Internet: www.matthiasmedia.com.au

Matthias Media (USA)
Telephone: 1-866-407-4530
Facsimile: 724-964-8166
Email: sales@matthiasmedia.com
Internet: www.matthiasmedia.com

Also from Matthias Media

About Pathway Bible Guides

Pathway Bible Guides are simple, straightforward, easy-to-read Bible studies, ideal for groups who are new to studying the Bible, or groups with limited time for study. We've designed the studies to be short and easy to use, with an uncomplicated vocabulary. At the same time, we've tried to do justice to the passages being studied, and to model good Bible-reading principles. Pathway Bible Guides are simple without being simplistic; no-nonsense without being no-content.

As at May 2010, the series contains the following titles:

- *Beginning with God* (Genesis 1-12)
- *Getting to Know God* (Exodus 1-20)
- *The Art of Living* (Proverbs)
- *Seeing Things God's Way* (Daniel)
- *Fear and Freedom* (Matthew 8-12)
- *Following Jesus* (Luke 9-12)
- *Peace with God* (Romans)
- *Church Matters* (1 Corinthians 1-7)
- *Standing Firm* (1 Thessalonians)

For more information or to order contact:

Matthias Media
Telephone: +61-2-9663-1478
Facsimile: +61-2-9663-3265
Email: info@matthiasmedia.com.au
Internet: www.matthiasmedia.com.au

Matthias Media (USA)
Telephone: 1-866-407-4530
Facsimile: 724-964-8166
Email: sales@matthiasmedia.com
Internet: www.matthiasmedia.com

Also from Matthias Media

The Daily Reading Bible

Time to get back into regular Bible reading? *The Daily Reading Bible* has everything you need to get started, in one compact, portable package.

Each volume contains around 60 undated readings. Each reading is designed to take around 15-20 minutes, and contains:

- the full text of the Bible passage for that reading
- some questions to get you thinking
- some 'points to ponder' and
- some ideas to get you started in prayer.

All this in one booklet that you can take with you anywhere—on the train, on the bus, to the park at lunchtime, or to your favourite armchair.

Vol	Contains readings from ...
1	Matthew 5-6, Joshua, 1 Corinthians 1-4
2	1 Corinthians 5-7, Malachi, topical passages about God's trinitarian characteristics
3	Genesis 1-11, 2 Thessalonians, Hebrews 1-7, topical passages about Jesus
4	Matthew 8-16, Nehemiah, Hebrews 8-13
5	James, Genesis 12-35, topical passages about the atonement
6	Ephesians, Lamentations, Proverbs
7	1 Peter, Zechariah, Revelation 1-3, topical passages about our present suffering
8	John 1-12, Hosea, topical passages about the power of words
9	John 13-21, Isaiah 1-12, Philippians
10	1 Timothy, Exodus 1-18, topical passages on the Christian calling
11	2 Peter, Genesis 36-50, Ecclesiastes, topical passages on the image of God
12	Elijah, Matthew 1-4, 1 Thessalonians
13	Luke 1-6, Amos, 2 Corinthians
14	Luke 7-9, Micah, Galatians
15	Luke 9-15, Jonah, 2 Timothy
16	Luke 16-19, Job 1-26, 1 Corinthians 8-16
17	Luke 19-24, Job 27-42, topical passages on church
18	Acts 1-9, Numbers, Colossians
19	Titus, Isaiah 13-27, topical passages on the Ten Commandments
20	Judges, topical passages on practical Christian living, Daniel

FOR MORE INFORMATION OR TO ORDER CONTACT:

Matthias Media
Telephone: +61-2-9663-1478
Facsimile: +61-2-9663-3265
Email: info@matthiasmedia.com.au
Internet: www.matthiasmedia.com.au

Matthias Media (USA)
Telephone: 1-866-407-4530
Facsimile: 724-964-8166
Email: sales@matthiasmedia.com
Internet: www.matthiasmedia.com